10 Little Rules
for Getting IT Done

by
Jenn Lorenz

ISBN: 979-8-9988281-6-4

Published by Little Rules Publishing

DEDICATION

I dedicate this book to the people who have helped to shape my life.

To all four of my parents, thank you. Having raised children of my own, I've come to realize there is no rulebook for parenting. You co-parented long before it was cool, and each of you supported me in your unique way. You all taught me how to work hard, appreciate what I have, and make time for the people and things I love. You each worked hard to pave the way for me to have a "better" life than yours, and for that, I am grateful.

To my siblings, thank you for always being there, even from afar; your support means the world to me. And to my "Asister," you are the perfect blend of assistant and sister rolled into one. Thank you for being my ride or die, never asking questions, and saving a few lives in the making of my life.

To my children, my love for you is infinite. Being your mom is my greatest joy. I am so proud of you both. Thank you for supporting my leap into new adventures, even if it changes your life.

To my in-laws and Granny, we may not be blood-related, but you have supported and loved me nonetheless.

I am lucky to have you all in my life.

ACKNOWLEDGEMENTS

When I was in elementary school, we would start the school year by writing a little summary about what we did over our summer vacation. My summer story this year is pretty noteworthy; I upended my otherwise comfortable life and embarked on a journey to start a business. I began with a brief vacation between the end of my 20-year career and Day 1 of my new business. That was the plan anyway – relax, travel a bit, meet up with old friends, and make new ones. Then I reconnected with Frank Winters, a former colleague, and my plans immediately changed in one 30-minute phone call! It was his suggestion, during our first call, recounting our stories, that I share some of mine with others. He planted the seed. He introduced me to Carol Pearson, who made my ramblings into a book worthy of reading. I laugh that my "how I spent my summer" story is now about writing this book; this wasn't even on my radar three months ago. It is funny how life works, and I appreciate people like Frank and Carol who are always willing to share their expertise and help others. Thank you, my friends, for showing the way.

Jenn Lorenz

FOREWORD

It was a quick email with a quirky subject line on a random afternoon that introduced me to Jenn and her ideas about getting things done. (Thank you, as ever, Frank Winters.) After our first call, I had zero doubts in my mind this book would happen ... mainly because of who Jenn is and how boldly she approaches the challenges in her life, including writing her first book. What I didn't realize at the time is how much *I* needed this book. I've been "getting things done" in good form for years ... still, her wisdom and examples made me look at my "why" in a whole new way. Because it's not just about the "doing" ... it's about approaching what needs to be done is a systematic way that manifests into alignment with one's true priorities and constantly raises the bar on how you approach ... life. I hope you'll feel the same way after you read it.

Carol Pearson
Founder & Publisher
Little Rules Publishing

Jenn Lorenz

CONTENTS

Jenn Lorenz

INTRODUCTION

This book is not about a new business idea or framework. Instead, it is a short read intended to leave you with some strategies that you can apply, both in your everyday life and in **business**, to problem-solve and achieve the results you want. These rules serve as mantras in my life, helping me remain calm and focused during times of feeling stuck or overwhelmed; these rules allow me to move forward. My hope is they will be helpful to you, too.

I've included some of the more interesting events and interactions with people I have had in my journey. Throughout my life, I always told myself that my older self would appreciate having good stories to retell when reliving her life. So far, I have succeeded in that mission. I'm just like anyone else; I have failed more than I have succeeded, but I can tell you I have had a lot of fun along the way. I wrote this book to share some ideas to help you get to where you're trying to go a little faster and without beating yourself up; I wrote this book for you. Take what you find helpful in my stories and adjust it to fit your own story, building your toolkit. Your confidence in yourself will grow, and you'll learn to better navigate whatever comes your way. More importantly, you'll know and believe – from the core of your being – that you can get it done.

Another fun note; the capitalization of 'IT' in the title is a clever play on the word 'it.' I use IT as a nod to how I stumbled into a career in the information technology field and flourished as a public servant, starting as an intern and rising to become an executive for one of the largest public sector IT agencies in the country throughout my 20-year career. Being in IT is a constant cycle of change, and by the time I started my career with the State of New York, I was navigating one of the most significant changes of my life. From then on, I honed my skills, challenging myself daily to do better in *all* aspects of my life. These rules are how I now live my life, and I hope by sharing them, I can save you a little bit of time and frustration on your own journey. The stories in the book are loosely based on events that occurred in my life. The names and details have been modified for entertainment purposes.

The title of each chapter is the name of each rule. Every chapter ends with space for journaling to help you think through your own scenario and contemplate how you might incorporate the rules next time you encounter a similar situation.

I've also included AI chat prompt suggestions at the end of each chapter; feel free to modify them to fit your needs. Focus on solving a problem and give it some context; this is more likely to get a helpful response. It's just a fun part of the exercise to show you some interesting ways to use AI chat and give you additional ideas to consider. I find that a good AI chat is similar to sitting with my human friends, getting their input and feedback. Just as you would when talking with your friends, you ultimately want to verify the information. Take the time to fact-check and confirm that the responses make sense to you. You are the one who ultimately decides how you'd like to proceed; AI is simply a tool to help you save time and spark new ideas.

Jenn Lorenz

RULE 1
Get IT Done

"Yeah, so what are you going to do about it?"

These words pulled me out of my pity party. I was on a long-distance phone call with my mom, who went on to remind me that I am not the first person – and certainly will not be the last – to get divorced. Right before this conversation, I was in a downward spiral, reconsidering all of my life choices, making an extra effort to find and dwell on my failures. As my mom delivered those words so matter-of-factly, I was snapped back to reality. I realized at that moment that even if I didn't have any answers, I was determined to figure out what I was going to do about it. Figuring it all out eventually became my call to action: Get it done.

I didn't know it then, but this significant change in my life would teach me more than I could have ever learned in school, because the full responsibility of what this new life would entail started and ended with me. Don't get me wrong; I wasn't new to life-changing events, nor was I afraid of them. I left home at 18 to join the United States Air Force; that certainly was a significant life change, but one that I wanted. I had been thinking and preparing for it for as long as I could remember. I expected and anticipated all the unknowns that could come with this decision; I knew I would have to adjust, and I did.

The divorce was different. I didn't have time to prepare, and I certainly wasn't excited or looking forward to all of the "new experiences." I didn't want my otherwise comfortable life to change. I had been operating under the assumption I would have a partner, the same partner, for the rest of my life. I didn't even know what it meant to make a new life. The future looked vast to me; I couldn't imagine what mine would be like, but I had to figure it out – I had to get it done. I had to make a new life for myself and my two children, ages two and four at the time. I had no choice; my life was changing, and I needed to figure out what that meant.

On its surface, "make a new life" sounds like a no-brainer. As my mom said, I am not the first person to go through this. Well, that may be true, but I didn't know what all of those other people knew. How did they do it? What did they do? I didn't have a guide in my grasp to help me transition from a divorced life to a new one. I didn't know where to start; the future looked daunting. I was living in Germany, having not worked in over a year, and I had two small people to consider in every decision I made; whatever I did also affected them. In my mind, the stakes couldn't be higher.

Before I could think about what I wanted, I had to get over the first hurdle, which was how I felt about the situation. I am generally not one to dive into feelings, but I can say that during this period, I was grieving the loss of all that could have been. I was sad for my children who would not live the life I had wanted for them, and I oscillated between agreeing that the divorce was, in fact, the right decision and searching for ways to make the marriage work – maybe we could separate but stay married for the kids, a scenario I can't even fathom today. This meant I had to decide what *I* wanted. I came to this conclusion by focusing on the healthiest option for myself and the children. I wanted a life filled with love, support, and stability.

As these objectives became clearer, it strengthened my desire for a new life, and I allowed myself to accept my new reality: I was jobless, had no college degree, had two small children, lived far away from home, would soon be without a place to live, and had no support system nearby. This all occurred during a time when online communication was still in its infancy. My support system was not readily available, even by phone, due to the time difference and the high cost of long-distance calls. When those famous words from my mom replayed in my head, I could see the answer for the first time: Move back home.

As "Yeah, so what are you going to do about it?" played like a record in my head, it worked in a strange way to keep all of the negative what-if scenarios from overtaking my mind. I was able to think, and my new answer became clear: "I am going to focus on what needs to be done immediately and plan only for the next three months." I told myself it was okay not to know everything right away; I would adjust once I was back home and had my bearings in this new reality. This permission alleviated so much pressure; I allowed myself to not know the answers and, more importantly, enabled myself to move forward.

Taking action to move home was certainly a big step, yet it was a calculated next step. It addressed many of my concerns, bought me time, and answered the question of where I would live, providing me and my children with a support system. All I had to do was pack our stuff and buy the plane tickets. I was also fortunate that the military handled the logistics of the move, alleviating another huge source of pressure.

The decision-making process was challenging; there were so many factors to consider. Yet as soon as I made the decision, I started to feel a sense of security, and it reminded me I am capable of doing this. The act of leaving made it real and provided an outlet for the negative energy, which propelled me forward in planning the rest of my new life.

Over time, I eventually learned that action is my version of a magic pill; it's like a physical release of energy that annihilates any fear or negative thoughts. When I encounter a situation that evokes feelings of doubt, anxiety, and negative emotions, and my internal messaging system is only relaying what could go wrong, I stop all the noise with the phrase "get it done," and bam, I'm back in reality. It's not easy to calm yourself and focus your attention during a tumultuous time, but it's vital to making good decisions. That's why I refer to these rules as mantras, which I say to myself to ground me and get my mind to a place where I can think.

As I've grown in wisdom, I've stopped spending time wondering how we got to a particular situation, skip past any emotional reaction, and lead with action as my first rule. Although I haven't perfected this ability, I save a lot of time by not dwelling on *why* things happened or *who's* responsible. Those details may be necessary to understand eventually, but I'll add them to the list of things to review once we've done what needs to be done.

Today, I focus my time and energy on the actions required to achieve my next goal.

On many occasions, work would evoke some of the same feelings in me that my divorce did. There would be turmoil whenever there were leadership changes or when the unit I was in experienced personnel changes, or when my boss gave new, unfamiliar directions. Additionally, work would often come to a standstill because the people involved couldn't agree on the next step. Even though the work changes were not necessarily as severe as what I went through during my divorce, it was a change, and the feelings were the same to me. In those situations, I often felt stuck or overwhelmed, which also meant I wasn't very helpful to the team. I started to do the only thing I knew how to snap out of those feelings, starting with the words of my mother: "What are you going to do about it?" The answer over time came more easily: "Get it done." Every single time, that put the noise and fear at bay, and I could think, focus on what action, what smallest step with the least amount of risk I could make to buy time, create positive energy, and hopefully generate a little momentum.

When working with teams, I would use the phrase "get it done," with the subtext of "legally, ethically, and responsibly," like the fine print that is read out loud very quickly during a medical commercial. This signaled to my coworkers, partners, employees, and other stakeholders that positive action is the only way forward.

We will not stop until the task, goal, objective, or other goal is complete, calculating and mitigating the risks along the way. Yes, those three words are concise and straightforward; by no means do they imply it's easy. More importantly, this phrase serves as a reminder to accept the situation as it is, to remove emotions from the problem, and to take action.

Jenn Lorenz

your turn...

Get IT done

Give yourself credit. On the following few pages, list two challenges you've encountered in your life. How did you feel? Did you know right away what outcomes you wanted?

What emotions did you have to overcome before you could accept the new reality and decide what action to take?

If you haven't used this "Get it done" approach before, would you consider trying it now as part of your strategy?

When you take an action, do you find it alleviates the fear and anxiety you have? Do you feel a little more in control?

AI Chat Prompt

Suppose you are contemplating significant changes in your life. A chat with an AI tool can provide valuable ideas to consider in your planning and help create checklists. If I had this tool available to me in preparing for my new life, I might have found a prompt like this useful:

A young adult, late twenties, with two children, faced with divorce, has no income and will lose their home. Create a strategy to help create a new life. What questions should a young adult ask? Create a checklist of things to do.

The results may not be entirely applicable to your situation; review them and adjust them to fit your needs. This definitely would have saved me time and helped me think through the possibilities, clearly and with less anxiety.

Jenn Lorenz

Jenn Lorenz

RULE 2
Do Your Homework

I look around the room, a little perplexed. Is everyone having the same reaction I am? Did our boss John just inform us that Michael, the unit head who reports directly to him, will be leaving the team today? Did John just name *me* the new unit head? My mind is spinning as it races through numerous questions, such as "What is going on?" and "Why didn't John give me a heads-up?"

I'm standing in a room full of people; not just any people, but my peers, and in this moment, I suddenly became their boss. What does it even mean to be a unit head? Also, why is this always happening to me? Just as quickly, queue the song from mom: "Yeah, so what are you going to do about it?" And if that's the hook, then the chorus has now become "This isn't the first time and won't be the last time."

Can anyone else hear this? Regardless, my inner self gave me the push to accept the situation as it was, and I bitterly acquiesce: Yes, I'll get it done. This is all happening in my head within the five-minute span of the conversation. No, I don't hear anything else John had to say. All I know is his office will be my first stop after this meeting ends. That is the smallest, least risky action I can take to address my concerns and gather more information.

Out of my head and back to the meeting, I am doing my best to present a sense of calm. This would have been so much easier had I been prepared. I force myself to remove the shock and awe from my facial expression, attempting to replace it with a non-reaction – nothing to see here, a "just another day at the office" type of look. I don't know why I am surprised; change is normal, and this is not the last time that my job would undergo a sudden change. I went through all of these thoughts and emotional changes in about 10 minutes: shock, awe, frustration, then acceptance. Once I had managed my emotional reaction, I quickly moved into a "let's get to work" mode.

Action had become my stress reliever, and I was ready to get going as these thoughts lingered in my head: What does it mean to be the unit head? What will be expected of me in this role? As my peers walk past me to leave the room, I answer random questions and thank those who congratulate me. The next smallest step I can take with the least amount of risk is to talk to the team. I am sure they are all just as shocked. I'll need to answer their questions and set my expectations, but before I can do that, I need to take a minute to get my bearings.

First stop? My boss's office for an honest conversation about what just happened and what he expects of me. I am using all of my words, but I am doing everything to appear calm, cool, and collected. Otherwise, I risk not getting any information and having this opportunity pulled away from me. As my boss, John doesn't owe me any answers, but we do have a good working relationship, and I know I can be honest. I want to maintain this relationship, so I am very aware of my emotions and do my best to keep them out of this.

"Jenn, sorry I did that to you. However, my morning began with an urgent call from my boss, asking me to get a project back on track by assigning one of our top leaders, in this case, Michael. It doesn't make it right, but Michael learned at the same time you did. He is outside waiting to talk to me. I just need your support in this. I chose you to be the next unit director because you have a general understanding of all the work in progress, and I know you'll be able to get up to speed and carry the team forward quickly. We can't have our in-flight work impacted by Michael's departure. Yes, this change is happening today, and I took advantage of the already scheduled morning meeting with the team to inform everyone at once. What I need to know now is, are you with me?"

"Yes, of course. I'm in," I replied without hesitation. "I appreciate being selected for this opportunity. We have previously discussed the ideas I have to enhance productivity and foster stronger relationships with our customers. But, I am curious, is that what you expect of me in this role?"

I could sense that John was short on time, and this was going to be a brief answer.

"We are in the middle of budget planning. I need the financial plan from the team ASAP. Yes, the other improvements you previously proposed can be included in the plans. However, you have about five minutes to determine if there is funding to support them. Thanks for stepping up; now get out so I can get to my next meeting."

I left John's office with more information than I had when I arrived. Although it wasn't all the answers I would need, I had enough to follow up with the team and get us back on track.

Next step: Meet with the team to hear their concerns and gain insight into their work. With each issue raised, I gained a better understanding of what the team expected from the role of unit head and realized I needed to strengthen my skills in a few areas. I acknowledged that I am not Michael; I didn't know how he did the job. All I could do was my best, which meant I needed to do my homework.

This would involve research and planning. In this case, I was uncertain about the expectations for the unit head role. I used the information provided by my boss and the team as the basis for my research. Additionally, I requested a copy of the job duties, description, and minimum qualifications for the position from the human resources office.

When leading a new team or taking on a job I haven't done before, I often visit the library to read books on the subject. My goal is to establish a baseline from which to work. As I conduct my research, I question whether I possess the necessary skills to complete the assigned tasks. If I lack specific skills, I recognize these gaps as areas I need to address.

In this scenario, where I was assuming the role of unit head, I excel in service delivery, continuous improvement, and productivity. However, I learned that the team had budget needs that were not being met, and some vendors were not honoring their obligations. I realized I needed to become more familiar with these areas.

I also understood I could not do all of the work on my own; still, I perform best when I at least grasp the team's needs and can distinguish my responsibilities from those of my staff. Fortunately, Michael was nearby and I was able to ask him about the budget and vendor management issues. He shared his perspective on the responsibilities of the unit head versus the staff, along with the goals he was focused on. This conversation provided a starting point and allowed me to maintain momentum within the team while giving me time to learn more. I knew I could adjust my approach as I moved forward.

I lean into doing my homework because I have witnessed fear, either within myself or others, bring projects and work to a halt. The fear of the unknown can be debilitating. Rather than give in to it, I use it as a source of fuel. I let it inform me of all of the risks to consider, and then I get to work. As my discussions with the team continued, I learned of a scheduled delivery of service to a new customer in two weeks. My first reaction is, "Are we ready?" I didn't know the answer, and we were short on time. To assuage this fear and channel my energy, I asked for access to the service, to test it myself as if I were an employee of the new agency. It was a short time frame, and I needed a crash course in what was being delivered and the quality. Testing allowed me to learn more about it and create some level of comfort. Next fear – do we have enough people to support the go-live? I ask for the go-live schedule and have the team educate the audience on the service. Each of these questions will lead to more questions, but this is the process I repeat over and over again until I've addressed as many of my fears as possible. I have thought about mitigation strategies and solutions for any fears I have. I rarely write these things down; I just think them through so I am prepared at the time of delivery. Doing this work up front allows me to keep things moving forward in the day-to-day of whatever has been thrown my way. The research, planning, and preparation that go into doing my homework give me the knowledge to combat my fears.

Doing the homework is the kryptonite I bring to every situation. Every time I can thwart the unknown by learning, making informed decisions, and, most importantly, taking the next best action, my confidence grows, and I can move more quickly next time. I became comfortable with the idea that when I didn't know the answers, I could figure them out, which brought me a sense of calm over the years that allowed me to lead with confidence. Acknowledging that no one has all the answers, everyone has a different approach, yet we can and will make informed decisions creates a sense of calm amidst the chaos.

I have always been fascinated by how others navigate the unknown and combat their fears during their own journey. I research champions in sports, the military, and business to learn about their preparation techniques. I found there were general themes, often around setting a goal and prioritizing it in their lives. Take, for example, a long-term goal like a 5K road race three months from now. Champions realize if they wake up on the day of the race without preparation and attempt to run at full speed, they will likely hurt themselves and not perform their best overall. Instead, they research and create a detailed plan that outlines how they will allocate their time each day leading up to the race in preparation. This kind of prep works for things that are out of our control, too. A runner may have anxiety about the weather conditions; researching how other runners prepared themselves for the same race can alleviate those fears and give them an advantage over those who may not know to bring gear for all types of weather.

Importantly, champion-level runners will research beyond running, including details about their diet and rest time, to help them meet their goal. This preparation involves specific research and planning, and using their findings to inform their approach. Once the direction is clear, they plan the necessary actions to achieve the goal.

Breaking up the work into daily goals is another way to combat the anxiety of the unknown. It will give you a sense of control; even if little things pop up that try to take your focus off the goal, you'll have a clearly defined action plan in front of you to help you stay focused and reach your destination.

Of course, there are times when the direction may be obvious, but the "how" you'll get there may seem unattainable because the steps from here to there are not obvious. For instance, after returning to New York State, I decided to go back to school. I had two small children and a job that consumed most of my time. Still, I realized having a degree was crucial for advancing my career, and I had to figure out how to make the time to pursue it. It wasn't easy; the schedules for the children and work often conflicted with school. I didn't know how I was going to juggle it all. To help me figure it out, I researched how other people managed their busy lives and met their goals. I found that most successful people prepared like champions, creating schedules that outlined daily tasks of what they would accomplish. Some schedules were even more detailed, specifying what to do in the hours or even minutes.

The structure of a schedule was helpful, but with two children it needed flexibility built in. I had two years left of school, and creating a two-year plan didn't make sense for me. I barely knew what was going to happen the next day, let alone commit to two years out. Instead, I chose to create a plan at the start of each semester. A schedule based on the semester allowed me to look ahead at the children's school and babysitter schedules, identify when they had planned time off, and plan my time off accordingly. Then, I created daily agendas tailored to the day's needs. I used my school syllabus to plan out my homework assignments, blocking time as needed, typically from 9 p.m. to 1 a.m., to ensure I stayed on task with my schoolwork. I blocked 5-8 p.m. for after-school activities with the children. I filled in my work schedule from there. As an hourly employee I had some flexibility, but I also needed the money, so I tried to work as many hours as I could. The children were my highest priority; their needs came first. School and work competed daily for second place. Household chores were assigned on a weekly basis, depending on the time I had left. Rather than completing all tasks every week, I picked a few to tackle each week. Again, it was about my priorities.

This schedule rarely became a daily routine; still, it was enough to guide me through each day. Some days the children didn't have a lot of after-school activities; I used that "extra" time to get ahead on homework if I was up against the clock for an assignment. Other days, our family time was spent on chores. The point is, the schedule served as a guide. After two years of this craziness, I did earn my college degree. The goal is to create some calm within the chaos, enabling you to keep moving in the direction you want. A general schedule provided me with a sense of stability. I was mentally prepared for potential bumps, and at the end of each day, even if the progress was minimal, I knew I was moving forward.

In my case, the experiences I gained through real-life events influenced my approach to my work life. As I joined state service and started to apply the things I've learned, I found those new skills so helpful in getting things done, which is definitely the space I like to be in. I feel much better when things make sense and they're moving along, when we're doing what we said we were going to do. I strive for that sense of accomplishment that comes with knowing what's next. I understand we might have some hurdles to get through, but I seek order.

For example, let's look at my goal of completing my degree. I had a two-year timeline to complete this degree, which seems like a long runway. I learned valuable skills through that daily routine, which I used for nearly two years. Trust me, it was at times utterly boring and painful, but it taught me the importance of tenacity and perseverance, regardless of the obstacles I faced. If you are going through similar challenges, stay focused. I had to go through it myself to trust this method, but it actually works. Just take one step at a time, be kind to yourself, and you will get there.

Now I'm translating this method to a business plan, preparing much like a champion would. First, I identified my big-picture goals, planned the work that supports them, and broke it all down into daily tasks and created routines. For instance, as the founder of a new company, one of my objectives was to publish this book within a few months, which necessitated completing the manuscript by the end of this month. According to my editor, the manuscript should be about 20,000 words long. On its surface, that's quite a daunting task. I have not written multiple pages in a professional format in more than a decade. To wrap my mind around this and help myself accept this reality, I had to break the work into chunks over time. There are roughly 30 days in the month, and we are about six days in. To break this down into a more manageable measure, I need to write approximately 1,000 words a day over the next 20 days to achieve my goal. I may need to reschedule personal appointments and skip a few family dinners to stay on track. However, knowing this daily goal gives me a structure to work from. I can plan and make decisions more accurately about how I spend my time and, most importantly, work to meet the goal.

The ability to see the big picture goal and break it down into smaller, tangible pieces is an overlooked and often under-appreciated skill. From my perspective, working without a plan is like running endlessly in a hamster wheel, staring at yourself in a mirror, wondering why you are not making progress. Can you imagine how frustrating that must be? Or maybe that's where you are, working like crazy but never feeling like you're making any progress. Instead, I prefer to prepare like a champion. I intentionally create a sense of order and calmness, knowing that challenges may arise along the way. I also imagine the feeling of joy that comes with crossing that finish line. Give yourself the time to think through what it will entail to achieve your goal and how great you'll feel when you get there!

As you build your plan, be sure to think about potential risks and challenges that could arise. I refer to these as "doomsday scenarios." Consider the worst-case scenario and put everything on the table. That's what my mom did; her goal was to raise us so we could survive anything. If one day only the cockroaches were left, she wanted us to be able to survive with them. She did a great job! While I will have to save all the ways we prepared for another book, I have come to realize her goal is not my goal, but the way we considered what could happen and prepared for it was a skill in itself, and it all came down to answering the question: "What are you going to do about it?"

Remember, there is no one-size-fits-all solution. Tailor your plan to fit your specific needs, inform it through research, and learn from others. Do this often, not just in times of crisis. Learning these skills does take effort and can be challenging, but if you stick to the plan most days, you will reach your goals.

You don't need to have all the answers; just having some thoughts about potential challenges will help reduce the shock when those inevitable obstacles arise in your daily plan. I am sure that by now, at this point in your life, you have already handled many challenges. I found child care to be one of the most difficult situations to navigate because there were so many variables; weather or illness would pop up and cause an unplanned shutdown of the daycare. Although it would have been preferable to have advance notice, it wasn't possible. And of course, this always seemed to happen on a Sunday going into Monday; many places are not open on Sunday, so planning for alternate care by 7 a.m. Monday was a bear. I also had concerns about how the children would handle the sudden change. This is how I'd talk myself through it: The kids may have to adjust to some changes, but I'll ensure they are safe wherever they are. They will also learn that change is normal, and while they may be nervous at first, when I pick them up at the end of the day, they'll remember those feelings were only temporary. On the positive side, we'll be building a new relationship with a backup sitter for next time. Yes, it's hard the first time, but it will get easier; just keep going.

your turn...

Do your homework

As you consider your goals, what fears hold you back? Write them down on the following pages – the good, the bad, and the ugly.

List out as many concerns as you can think of. Then ask yourself how much of your fear is based on the unknown?

Perhaps a goal of yours is to be the next unit head, but the total value of the unit budget is more than that of a small state. You are intimidated by it. Ask yourself why.

Then consider what you can do to prepare yourself to handle large budgets in the future. Write down the various courses you can take, or identify a colleague who can help to mentor you, perhaps ask your boss to let you listen in on budget planning meetings so you can start to learn the language and see the negotiations in real time.

AI Chat Prompt

Let's take the scenario where a person has a goal to become a unit head. A significant responsibility of the unit head is to manage a large budget. The person interested in the role lacks the qualifications to perform the duties. AI can provide some ideas to help prepare someone for achieving their goal, with a prompt like this:

Imagine you are an individual aspiring to be a unit head, responsible for managing a large budget. Create a comprehensive training plan to develop the necessary skills and knowledge. Include certifications that may be useful in setting the individual apart from others. Summarize typical career paths and on-the-job training for individuals who become unit heads.

Review the results; if you find the response too broad, refine the prompt within the same chat to be more specific. For example, if the prompt proposes project management certification, you can respond with another prompt to ask which project management certification is most recognized, and ask for a link to a website. AI is simply saving you time by recommending a way forward. It is up to you to modify it to fit your needs. Use the following pages for your thoughts and notes.

_____

_____

_____

_____

_____

_____

_____

_____

_____

_____

_____

_____

_____

_____

Jenn Lorenz

RULE 3
Do the Work of Winning

My dad often reminded me that success is not an accident; it is the end result of all the time and effort you invest. Living each minute of your day with a focus on achieving your goals is essential. I frequently reference sports champions, who exemplify the ability to confront setbacks head-on. They acknowledge their challenges, learn from their experiences, and concentrate on their next steps. What defines a champion in my eyes is their go-to response to the questions "Okay, what are you going to do about it?" Their answer is simple: "Get it done."

Like everyone else, champions experience loss, make sacrifices, and encounter feelings of failure. They may also struggle with negative self-talk. However, the most significant difference lies in their ability to adapt and stay committed to their goals. They persevere and keep moving forward.

As I mentioned in Rule 2, completing the homework allowed me to adjust my daily routines. I have a few of them – my morning routine involves reflecting on the most important tasks I need to accomplish that day, mentally preparing myself for the day ahead, which I already know can get hectic. When I was in college, my morning routine typically included checking my syllabus and homework goals for that day. It served as a reminder of the time block I had set and helped navigate the rest of the day to ensure that my school time block was not hindered.

My morning accountability routine itself isn't time-consuming; it only takes about a minute. I make sure to ground myself by confirming what day it is: "Is it Tuesday? What's the actual date? Is it the 12th or the 16th?" This helps me put the day into perspective and maintain a running list of tasks that need to be done. As the day's events unfold, I can adjust my plans accordingly. I wake up, get physically ready, and make it a point to prepare mentally as well.

I also do a self-check in the evening; this takes about 15 minutes. I ask myself questions like, "Did I accomplish the things I wanted to do today? Did I have to postpone any homework? Do I need to readjust my schedule to compensate for that time? Did anything unexpected happen that requires me to reassess my plans? For example, did I just get a reminder about a doctor's appointment tomorrow that I completely forgot about?"

I have found the busier I am, evaluating my standing both in the morning and evening are actions that keep me focused and on track. The outcome of each day helps me understand the potential impact for tomorrow and the days to come. Am I still on track? Is there anything I need to remove from my to-do list or postpone to ensure I meet my goals? I must submit my homework on time, arrive at work punctually, and take care of my children. However, I might decide that vacuuming the entire house can wait until the weekend – priorities can shift based on my daily needs. I am shifting my focus each day to ensure the most critical tasks receive my full attention and are consistently completed, regardless of any obstacles that arise.

I have also found self-checks very helpful for measuring progress against the larger goal. Let's take the goal of completing my degree in two years. The school prescribed a total number of credits necessary for the degree. In order to successfully complete those credits, I needed to take and pass a number of various courses. I had given myself a two-year timeline to complete all of the coursework and broke that work out by semester, estimating I would need to take eight semesters' worth of work. Measuring my progress was straightforward; at the end of each semester, my grades determined whether

I had passed or failed. It was all there in black and white. Measuring by semester made progress very simple, because I was working with single digits, and progress was very clear: 1 of 8 semesters completed, 7 more semesters to go. This activity also served as a motivator. When day-to-day life got hard, which it often did, I would remind myself of the progress made, the hard days I had already made it through, and refocus my thoughts on getting to 8 of 8 semesters completed.

You can imagine that after navigating two years of intense scrutiny over my daily routine and constant self-created pressure to get my life in order, it was only natural these skills stayed with me and developed throughout my career. Doing the work of winning is a constant focus on making progress. It includes ongoing preparation and adjustment to navigate all of the obstacles that will inevitably happen.

One of the ways I like to prepare myself for any potential impending doom is to look at history. What I am doing in my life is not new, and there is no reason for me to reinvent the wheel. As a lifelong learner, I have always been fascinated by how others endured the struggles in their lives. I am curious to know about the choices they made when everything seemed against them. How did they navigate societal expectations? Did they choose a path for the greater good or for self-preservation? Why? What would I do if I encountered a similar scenario?

I find it fascinating how much the world has changed, yet there are always similarities between the past and the present. As I learn more, I will ask myself, "If they could do that, then I can certainly handle whatever I'm facing." This immediately changes my perspective and allows me to think about what is possible, rather than focusing on everything that is going wrong or dwelling on how far away my goal seems to be.

One of my favorite stories is that of an Irish chieftain from the late 1500s and early 1600s who gave Queen Elizabeth I of England a run for her royal money. This remarkable leader, known as the Pirate Queen, was Grace O'Malley. It was an intriguing time, as both women were breaking barriers in their complex roles in predominantly male-dominated societies. When I reflect on my own struggles, I find it hard not to draw comparisons to their extraordinary experiences.

To help paint the picture, both of these women lived in male-dominated societies. Women were not typically viewed as decision makers, especially when they were young. They both lost their fathers at a young age and became responsible for carrying on their family legacies. At the same time, they contended with threats daily from their own family members seeking to kill them to gain power, as well as political rivals. The world itself was harsh; indoor plumbing and electricity had yet to be invented, and at best, they resided in cold, damp castles. Additionally, the Pirate Queen was a skilled captain and led raids on other ships and on land, constantly asserting her abilities and power.

Unlike Queen Elizabeth 1, the Pirate Queen had children. Her husband was killed early in her reign, and she proceeded to raise her children while fighting off English colonization and ensuring her clan was fed, while defending against other chieftains and relatives trying to undermine her. This puts any struggles I have faced into stark perspective. She put in the work every day against odds I can't even fathom, and she did so over a 40-year reign. Stories like this are what motivate me when I need a reminder to do the work.

The English Crown viewed Grace O'Malley as a significant obstacle to their colonization efforts. In an attempt to bring her to the negotiating table, they captured her son. O'Malley requested an invitation for an audience with the Queen. This was unheard of at the time; chieftains were viewed as a lesser class than English royalty. However, the Queen agreed to meet and negotiate in person. Do I wish I could have been in the room that day! Keep in mind the only way to get from Ireland to Surrey, England, where the meeting was held, was over water. Depending on the weather, the journey could have taken anywhere from a couple of days to a week. The Queen had to be impressed to some degree. She was also a woman of great power, but she did not participate in warfare; she did not captain ships. Still, she faced many of the same challenges, as she also operated in a male-dominated political landscape. Their lives were not the same, but they both had lost their fathers at early ages and had to take on responsibilities they may not have even wanted to in the name of protecting the family legacy. The parallels are worth investigating further.

In life and in business, your ability to complete the tasks you have laid out for yourself can be directly or indirectly affected by others. You may encounter individuals who are purposefully trying to thwart your plans, as Grace discovered, which brings us to the next point about doing the work of winning. Negotiation will most likely be necessary to achieve the results you desire. In my earlier years, I often negotiated time off schedules with day care providers, advocated for more time to complete assignments with my college professors, and traded days off with colleagues to ensure I could meet my daily goals.

I appreciate Grace's story because she was not afraid to negotiate. It was an action she needed to take to achieve the results she wanted, and she was, in fact, successful in the negotiations; she secured the release of her son. She also had the gumption to push the envelope and advocated that the Queen acknowledge her position as Chieftain and allow her clan to keep operating at the local level. The English Queen agreed, but the Pirate Queen had to agree to adhere to English rule in return and pledge her loyalty to the Crown. However, once the

Pirate Queen returned to her homeland, she didn't make any effort to honor the agreement. She continued to show courage and prioritized the needs of her clan and asserted her authority against the English Crown.

Not only is this story fascinating for the period in which it occurred, with the political and everyday life challenges faced by both women, but it also includes lessons that we can learn from today. Clearly, the Pirate Queen knew her value and believed in her capabilities.

While there is some folklore around Grace O'Malley, she was a real person, and these events did happen. When I think about her life, and then I think about mine, I just ask myself, "Really, what did *you* do today?"

All kidding aside, the past provides lessons that will save us time and energy and assuage some of our fears if we just apply them to whatever situation we are facing. Grace's story happened hundreds of years ago, yet there are so many relatable aspects to our lives today. She had to balance the needs of her clan, the needs of her family, and plan for the future. I found her gumption to request a meeting with the Queen and her strategy for negotiating the return of her son impressive. If she can muster up the courage to request a meeting, in person, with the highest leader, who is constantly attacking her, I can certainly muster up the courage in my own life to request a meeting with decision makers who can help me get it done, whatever that may be.

When preparing for a negotiation, I consider the outcomes I want to achieve. In the context of getting it done, I think about the actions that need to happen. If I have determined there is a person or team that can help to get it done, I consider what is important to them. Is there anything in my request that will help them move forward? Consider what the other side will expect in return. I do my best to understand who I am negotiating with. In a situation as serious as advocating for the well-being of your child, showing up in person may be necessary.

Considering what counteroffers I'd be willing to accept and how I plan to counter is also part of the preparation. In the context of getting it done, my number one goal is staying on time. The give and take of the negotiation is based on how much time I can gain or avoid wasting if I am successful in the negotiation. Thinking through the conversation beforehand, considering the format of the meeting, is also helpful to minimize or eliminate some of the fear around the conversation or negotiation. When I think through these scenarios before the main event, I am more able to remain calm and have confidence during the negotiation, adapting to the ebb and flow of the conversation to get to an agreeable outcome.

In doing the work of winning, sometimes the only person who can get the job done is you. Depending on the leadership and business management rules you read, you'll learn a lot about the importance of delegation and getting the right people in place at the right time. While this is true, there may be situations where there's no one to delegate to. It may be necessary, due to the urgency of the problem, that you step in and do the work yourself.

Let's revisit the Pirate Queen's story for context. She arrives at a juncture in her life where she plans to hand leadership of the clan to her son. She chose a significant battle with the English as the opportunity to announce him and delegated to him the task of leading the O'Malley clan into the battle. However, when he arrives on the scene, he does not follow the orders given to him and chooses to join the English, much to the disappointment of the other clansmen and his mom. To say her plan to hand over the reins failed is an understatement. As a result of his failure to obey orders, the Pirate Queen had to rectify the situation by attacking his castle. This sent a clear message to the English, the larger O'Malley clan, and other clans that the O'Malleys were not joining the English. Perhaps this all would have been avoided if she had not delegated in the first place.

The Pirate Queen shows us it is difficult to determine when to delegate and to whom. I have found that getting directly involved is most helpful when joining a new team, when time is of the essence, or when change is necessary. Then I become hands-on with the work. Once the ball is rolling, the next step is to teach others.

It remains true that empowering as many people as possible to serve as a multiplier in doing the work makes the most sense; nobody can do it on their own, nor is that the expectation. However, that isn't always possible. When deciding what to hand off, consider urgency, relationships, level of expertise, and risk.

Part of delegation is paying attention to how your team is spending their time. Remember a time when you sat in a meeting and thought to yourself, "Why am I here?" Imagine your team of 10 is thinking the same thing during a 60-minute meeting. That's potentially 600 wasted minutes. A remedy for this is requiring clear agendas that include the purpose for the meeting, the expected outcome of the meeting, and the questions or topics that need to be addressed to inform the outcome. I prefer to take it a step further and include the name of each person speaking and the time that will be spent on each topic. This is useful when planning for larger meetings where the participants may not know each other. While the agenda is helpful in making it clear how everyone will spend their time in the meeting, it is just as important to give the participants enough time to prepare. This really makes a big difference. When everyone knows why they're there and what they're meant to contribute, meetings feel more productive – and it's easier for people to feel like their time is valued.

Also, I found it helpful to pay attention to what people say and do. Consider the phrase " the slow roll." This is the scenario where, as the leader, you will hear a lot of agreement. It will sound and feel like there's energy, but when you do your daily check-in for progress, you're not seeing the results you expect. The people you're working with are saying "Yes, I'm working on it," "Yes, I am done," or "Yes, we're working together," yet you don't see results. That means you're not getting all of the information, and it's time to dig in and look deeper. In my opinion, digging deeper is a responsibility of a leader who should operate as an honest broker. If someone is conveying that work is getting done or tasks are in fact completed, that should mean *all* of the pieces are in fact done. I look for actual progress being made toward the goal; movement alone ... the slow roll ... does not equal results.

The work of winning also means determining what work can be completed in parallel and simultaneously. I had typically done enough homework to see not only the big picture but also have a good understanding of the financial tracks, the various work efforts, and how the human resources needed to be engaged. While there was interdependence amongst the tracks, there were tasks that could be accomplished within each without waiting on the other. For example, team members may need specific training before the next phase of the project can begin. Rather than stopping all work to train all the assigned people, allow three or four of the best people to spend 25% of their time on training. Ramp up their training time as the first phase of the project comes to a close. They'll be the leads for the next phase, while the remaining team will support the rollout of the first phase. There are a million ways to run tasks in parallel; the point is to find what works for you.

Remember, success is not an accident; it requires work every day. Embrace the obstacles; consider them excellent practice for the next time. Your confidence will grow as you overcome challenges, others will start to look to you for guidance, and you'll feel a growing sense of freedom. I found that I earned the ability to make decisions and effect change with little oversight as my skills and confidence grew. You may even have a little fun doing it!

Celebrate your success; forward motion is progress, no matter how small. Acknowledge the good you are doing and share your appreciation with your team, friends, or family for their support throughout the journey. I think this part is often overlooked; in my opinion, it is way more fun to talk about the things that are going well, the challenges that have been overcome, and what is coming on the horizon, rather than dwelling on all that went wrong and what cannot be changed.

Jenn Lorenz

your turn...

Do the work of winning

Sticking to a routine can be difficult. Write down three obstacles that could prevent you from staying on track. What adjustments would you have to make to persevere? How will you stay motivated to do the work each day?

Use the journaling space on the following pages to write your thoughts.

AI Chat Prompt

When I was planning my activities by day to help manage the competing priorities of work, family, school, and my household, I did it manually, creating lists and writing things down on a calendar. It took a lot of effort. Had I been able to chat with AI, I would have saved a lot of time and perhaps learned of possibilities I hadn't considered. A chat prompt that may have been helpful could be this:

A primary caregiver of two small children is working and completing college. Review the syllabus, work schedule, household chore list, and daycare calendar that were uploaded, and create a daily plan of activities that will ensure the coursework is completed on time while also accounting for care on the days the child care facility is closed. Suggest options for managing the coursework and create a list of proven motivational techniques that primary caregivers can use as a source of encouragement to complete their daily tasks. Include ideas for celebrating small wins to serve as a regular reminder that progress is being made.

Uploading your own documents in AI chats for reference saves so much time and gives you plenty of flexibility to adjust the conversation to your specific needs. Always check the results and modify them to fit your needs. Delete and start over as many times as you want. Remember, this is just one more tool to help you get it done.

Jenn Lorenz

Jenn Lorenz

RULE 4

Ignore More Than You Do

This is one of my favorite rules, and it's one of the most difficult for me to apply, especially when there are so many things competing for my time.

According to the Merriam-Webster dictionary, the meaning of ignore is to refuse to take notice of something or reject it as unimportant. Refusing to take notice of unimportant things sounds like a good time and energy saver to me. This is a little bit different, however, from deciding you are simply not going to do something. I learned this nugget of wisdom about time management from my father, who is far more disciplined than I. As a vice president for a large insurance firm, he mastered the skill of time management. I was lucky enough to bear witness to his journey and pick up some critical tidbits along the way.

In this rule, we're talking about the distractions that pop up throughout the day. Of course there will be urgent matters that arise that need to be addressed; those should not be ignored. What I am talking about here are the non-urgent distractions. As you know, I am accustomed to scheduling my day based on the priorities of the day. To stay on task, I ignore many of the notifications from internal social channels, email, news, and phone calls. Ignoring, in this case, means I literally refuse to take notice. I do not even spend the time to review it at the moment, and I skip making a decision of yes or no.

What I found is that many of these distractions resolve themselves in due time. Should something become a problem, it will come to me through the paths I have implemented to address issues quickly.

Let's say I receive an email notification as a courtesy copy about a water fountain that is not working in one of the 200 locations my staff works from. I ignore it. There are more than enough leaders from my team on the email to resolve it. I do not need to stop to write back or take any action. I also could have gone forever without reading that email, and I bet the issue would have been resolved. In the event this situation became a health and safety problem that my team could not handle, then I would be engaged by the facilities team if they needed support.

Perhaps one could argue that if I tackled the distraction the first time it swirled into my orbit, it wouldn't get bigger. That may be true, but that would also mean I stopped doing what I had planned to and delayed the results I intended to achieve. For me, that trade of time and energy is not equal in return. Assuming the distraction will become something bigger only creates fear about an unknown that cannot be measured. From my perspective, this type of worry is just a time sink and an energy waster. Tackle the issues when they are truly issues, and exploit opportunities when they are actual opportunities. Focus your energy on actions that keep you on track to get it done.

Jenn Lorenz

your turn...

Ignore more than you do

Think about how you spend your energy and time. Write down the top three things distracting you from your goals. Do you answer your phone every time it rings? Do you have notifications turned on for social media or news alerts?

What tools or practices could you use to reduce that noise and keep yourself focused? Use the journaling pages to jot down your thoughts.

AI Chat Prompt

Knowing what to ignore can be challenging in itself. Your journal entries have helped you consider what you could ignore going forward. The idea is that thinking about what you will ignore ahead of time will help you avoid distraction. Yet, it may still be difficult to decide what can be ignored. I have found decision trees very helpful in contemplating the outcomes of the choices I am making.

Let's stay with the scenario that a primary caregiver is attending school in the evenings, caring for children when day care is not available, handling house duties, and working during the day. The AI chat prompt may look like this:

A primary caregiver of two small children is working, completing college, managing household duties, and caring for the children whenever day care is not available. Create a decision tree as a guide to help the primary caregiver determine what can be ignored versus what needs to be acted on.

Rework this prompt to be relevant to your situation, and review the results. If you find the decision tree useful, consider it another tool to use when determining which direction to take. At the end of the day, the decisions are yours; the AI chat tool provides suggestions for you to modify to fit your needs or discard altogether.

Jenn Lorenz

Jenn Lorenz

RULE 5
Lead, Follow, or Support Others

You may know the saying "Lead me, follow me, or get out of my way," attributed to General George S. Patton, one of the most successful generals of the US Army. His point was that he was literally on a mission. He's trying to get it done, and those are the only options for those around him. He's letting everyone know he's moving forward, with or without them. While I did not have the same experiences as the general, there were major projects and organizational change activities where the delays were so significant that applying Patton's rule was the only way to make progress. At the same time, it is an aggressive approach, even sometimes uncaring, but it can be necessary when the goal is to get it done. While I understand and appreciate this approach, I've found it more effective to bring others along whenever possible.

Patton's mantra is a statement outward to others. I modified it slightly to be a guide for managing myself. Thinking about it in the context of "What are you going to do about it," my answer is to get it done by leading, following, or supporting others.

I say this for a couple of reasons, including the fact that I don't like to sit idly by. It's in my nature to want to be of value, especially in support of the greater good. I prefer to be of service and help others feel successful. I love the struggle of pushing towards improvement and making things better each time around, so when I see others working to achieve something, I am happy to lend my support.

There's a satisfaction that comes from being a part of moving a project forward, accomplishing a goal, or helping others reach theirs. With that in mind, at this stage of my life and career, when I am asked to be the lead, or even if I am in a situation where there is no decision maker and the rules are unclear, I am happy to step up or step into the unknown. I'll take the lead whenever the opportunity is presented. These days, I prefer to face the unknown rather than endure a crisis created by poor planning and poorer execution. I've learned how to handle myself in these situations, and I now know it's okay not to know everything. The main objective is to dive in with curiosity, see what's going on, and then make a path forward. Webster's dictionary defines leadership as going before or showing the way, and that's the space I prefer to be in.

Conversely, if an effort requires that I play the role of follower to get it done, then I will do so. Remember, my answer to "what are you going to do about it?" is "get it done." I don't get into petty nuances of who is or isn't doing more than someone else, or who gets the credit. Those three words – get it done – force me to hone in on the actions needed to achieve the results. When I encounter a situation where the direction is clear, someone else is leading, decisions are being made, and I am asked to get on board and support, I'm happy to lean in and do the work.

This is not always easy. I do not always agree with someone else's perspective on how something should get done; putting my personal opinion to the side takes effort. However, after being the leader of numerous organizational changes that affected thousands of people, implementing and operating computer systems that affect the millions of residents of New York, I know firsthand that the leader is carrying an extra burden. The stakes are typically high, and charting a new path is constantly scrutinized, not only within an organization but often publicly as well, adding to the pressure. As the leader, I can usually see where we need to go, and I'm grateful when those choosing to follow do so in an active way, completing tasks, informing the leader of risks, and creating solutions to mitigate those risks. Therefore, in a situation where I am the follower, I tell myself the leader gets two votes and we all get one. The leader is taking the shots; the very least I can do when asked to support is make it easier for the leader by doing what is asked of me.

I could argue that getting out of the way is, in fact, a method of supporting others, but I have become action-oriented. Rather than sitting idle, I'll serve as an advocate for the effort, sharing progress with my network, serving as a coach or mentor, or using my network to help remove roadblocks. My efforts may not always pan out, but there is no harm in trying. By supporting others, I am able to effect change, ideally more quickly, and I may even be helping others grow in their journey. Getting out of the way may be effective in getting it done, but supporting others gets it done in a meaningful way.

your turn...

Lead, follow, or support others

Think about a time in your life or career when something needed to be done, yet no one was taking the lead. Did you volunteer to be the lead during that time?

If you didn't, did you learn anything in this chapter that you would have applied to that scenario? Do you think the outcome would have been different? Would you have achieved the outcome sooner?

AI Chat Prompt

AI chat prompts can be used to contemplate business or life situations. Let's consider a scenario where a supervisor is struggling and doesn't fully understand the roles and behaviors of a leader, follower, and advocate. The supervisor could potentially use an AI chat prompt like this to create a comparison between the roles and gain insight into the differences:

Act as a supervisor who wants to learn more about the role and behaviors of a leader, follower, and advocate. Create a table for comparison that describes the role, the behaviors, the pros and cons of each, include a column to cite the reference with a link to the URL, and provide a two to three-sentence summary of when the role is most useful in the success of achieving goals, either in life or at work.

As always, review the chat results and use additional chat prompts to add clarifying details for your own situation and verify the information.

Use the journaling pages to write down your thoughts and ideas for moving forward.

Jenn Lorenz

Jenn Lorenz

RULE 6
Say What Needs to Be Said

"Team, the expectation is that we need this system back up in less than an hour. Our employees are not receiving deposits directly to their bank accounts. This situation is very concerning. Many have automatic debits scheduled to occur today, and they are concerned the funds won't be there, as I am. We will issue a communication informing them that we expect to have the system operational within the hour. Additionally, we will inform them a fail-safe mechanism is in place to retry the debits within 24 hours before fully failing the transaction. What I need to know immediately is what you need to bring the system up successfully." Translate this to the team: "What are you going to do about it? Get it done."

While most of the team stared at me blankly, I heard a quiet voice from the center of the room: "One suggestion, check that the invoice from the payroll processor has been paid. The payroll processor informed me and Jack four weeks ago that if the bill wasn't paid, they'd shut off services. This may be solved just by paying the bill."

A few other people start to chime in randomly and speak over each other: "Why wouldn't we pay a bill? Do we have the money to pay the bill? Why wouldn't you guys tell someone? Who didn't pay the bill? How did this happen?"

I stayed focused on the issue at hand: "Everyone, we have a major issue underway right now. We will discuss how we arrived at this point after we resolve this issue. We need everyone, yourselves included, to receive their direct deposits by the close of business. That's the goal. Let's get it done."

Saying the words – get it done – snapped everyone back to the present. By taking action to interrupt the banter, I was able to redirect the energy that was being spent on things we could not change to spending it on resolving the issue.

"Rick, thank you for bringing that to our attention," I continued. "You saved us a lot of time. We still need to fact-check. Mary, please call the payroll processor immediately and get back to me. Mark, let me know what the technology team is seeing on their side."

Fifteen minutes later: "Jenn, this is Mary. I called the payment processor. Rick was right; the invoice has not been paid for three months. I explained the current situation, and they told me that once they receive payment, they'll enable the services again. Can we go ahead and make the payment now?"

"Yes, Mary, pay the bill and get Mark on a call with the payment processor to get the direct deposits started today."

Half an hour later, Mary popped her head into my office: "Jenn, services are coming back online. Our staff are seeing their direct deposits."

"Thank you, Mary. Let's inform all of the employees that the system is back up. Work with the communications director to disseminate this information. I would like it to be shared as soon as possible to alleviate concerns. Please note that everyone can expect to receive their direct deposits by the close of business today. Then, select two people, one from finance and one from technology, to address staff questions or handle any issues that arise. We may have employees whose direct deposit is currently in limbo due to this issue, and I would like them to receive their payment as soon as possible. On the technology side, confirm with Mark that he is proactively identifying and resolving any errors on his end. I expect that some employees will still have difficulties; therefore, the two people you choose to provide support must be the best. I want our team to know that we take this seriously and will work directly with each of them until each issue is resolved. In the communication, provide the help desk number and have the two people you select manage the team, ready to respond to questions in the next 30 minutes. We have about two hours left in the day, and I want this all buttoned up before the end of the business day."

Two hours later, Mary is back in my office with an update. "Thank you, Mary. I am relieved to hear that all transactions are processed and every employee has been made whole."

The scenario I outlined is loosely based on real-life events. There are numerous reasons why an issue with direct deposit may be occurring, and just as many ways to resolve it. However, the point is not the details of the technology issue, but instead it is about the communication that occurred to rally the team to resolve the problems and get it done.

In this scenario, I play the role of Jenn, the owner of a small business. The direct deposits are failing for my employees. I have convened the team and immediately started the meeting by setting the expectation to bring the system back up in less than one hour. Saying it out loud focused the attention of the room and allowed everyone to think about how they can contribute to meeting the expectation.

I also found clarity in the message to be essential. Time and energy can be saved if you are as clear as possible and focus on what you want to accomplish, including a timeline. In this case, the expectation is to bring the system back online. The timeframe of less than an hour establishes urgency. As the team thinks through what actions they can take, the urgency informs them to expend as much energy as possible, meaning adding more people or tools, to solve the issue within the given time frame. It helps set the priority for allocating work.

In your own communications, open the channels by asking for thoughts and ideas from the team. Support and encourage these ideas, even if you will not proceed in that direction. In this case, it was probably intimidating for Rick to raise the possibility that a bill may not have been paid in front of his peers and leadership. Yet by doing so, he saved everyone time and avoided wasting energy on work that would be fruitless. Reward this behavior with positive encouragement. While it's possible Rick didn't do something he was supposed to, which led to the issue today, the focus right now is on fixing what is broken. If Rick didn't share this information, who knows how long it would have taken to get to a resolution?

While I titled this chapter Say What Needs to Be Said, it is worth noting that I have found communicating by action to be very useful as well. In the previously mentioned scenario, when the team conversation started to get a little panicky and people began throwing random questions and accusations in the air, I jumped in to redirect the conversation; sometimes it's OK to interrupt. That action broke the negative energy and redirected it. In situations where that doesn't resolve the issue, I'll ask the negative energy or energies to speak to me directly and separately. I may even ask that they do not rejoin the team setting until they can participate in a professional, respectful manner. I try to use time with the team to give clear instructions, and consistently help refocus them to spend their time and energy achieving results or making small progress.

This scenario is one example of a few key points that can be applied whenever something needs to get done, whether personal or business-related. Set expectations, be clear, foster the sharing of ideas, adjust as new information is learned, focus energy on what to do, and communicate with all who need to know clearly and often.

your turn...

Say what needs to be said

Communication helps create a sense of direction and fosters calm amongst the chaos. Think of situations you have experienced where clearer communication could have saved time, reduced confusion, and redirected energy towards results. Write down what or how you would communicate differently on the journaling pages.

AI Chat Prompt

Consider the scenario described above; the employees of a small business are concerned they are not receiving their direct deposits as expected. The owner of the business is requesting that communications be clear and sent with each update. AI can speed the delivery of messages by drafting the messages for review by the content owners. A chat prompt based on the request of the small business owner could be this:

Draft an email and a shorter message for the internal social channel informing employees that the issue causing direct deposits to fail had been resolved. If anyone is experiencing any additional problems receiving direct deposit, please contact the help desk at 555-555-5555. Review the drafts and edit them to fit your message.

While AI can draft the messages and send them on a schedule, it is vital that humans review the message before it is sent, and humans decide the schedule. Situations can change in a matter of seconds; the owner of the message should only use the draft as a suggestion, reviewing it and modifying it to ensure it is a clear, quality message. AI chat is only a tool; the results should not be considered the final copy.

Jenn Lorenz

RULE 7
Always Be Learning

"Yes, ma'am, that's correct. We have a computer system, and we are not using it to track room bookings or receive payments. We are using multiple books, which contributes to duplicate bookings, and customers have expressed significant frustration over this issue. Additionally, the financials are not reconciled, so our reports should not be trusted.

"No, Ma'am, I do not have experience with computers."

"Yes, Ma'am, I will figure it out."

These were my responses to the director of the Air Force base recreation center when she called me into the office to inquire about the status of our payment system and why customers were calling her in anger. She was a force to be reckoned with, and although a civilian in title, she carried herself as if her rank was commander; she had zero problem reminding you of her authority. Essentially, answering anything other than "yes, I will get it done" would be a bigger problem. This work effort had just become my single most important job. The director had the base commander on speed dial. Being the only military member at the recreation center, this assignment is mine, and the expectation is I will ensure its success. I'm not sweating yet; I am blissfully ignorant of what lies ahead. I couldn't have been more excited to jump in. After all, who doesn't love saving the day or, in this case, the business?

I was about three years into my military career, stationed in Okinawa, Japan, assigned to the Services Squadron. I was trained to support the dining facility and food service, lodging management, fitness centers, and community events planning. I began my career as a cook/baker during my three years stationed in the United Kingdom. When I arrived in Okinawa, I worked in a warehouse, operating a forklift that could lift loads to four stories in the air, and handled both incoming and outgoing deliveries. About a year later, I took a position supporting the base recreation center. We planned community events, such as the airshow, a complex undertaking, and hosted smaller events like bingo and casino nights at the recreation center. We also rented rooms for a small fee. We were a small team of fewer than 10 people; the rest of the staff were American civilians or Japanese residents.

This new task piqued my curiosity. What was preventing the use of the system? Why hasn't anyone mentioned this computer isn't meeting their needs? Who is responsible for the system? After speaking with the staff, I discovered they were using the books to track everything due to the complexity of the computer system, which they had not been adequately trained on. The computer appeared one day, and they experimented with it. However, their work procedures, which had not been updated to guide daily use, remained unchanged. Okay, this was a good problem. Based on my training, I knew how to run facilities, manage staff, plan and direct work, and update operating procedures, which is a regular event in the military; all work is scripted. I just needed the information. I'd train myself, update it, and then teach the staff. It sounds simple, right?

Wrong! When the staff said there was no training, they meant it. The actual paperwork with the computer was an overview of installing the application, but that's not training material. It's similar to the instructions you receive when assembling something. It is a book of information, but it focuses on the act of setting it up, rather than using it afterward. Fine, no big deal. I've got this. I'll just call the IT department; they'll have more information. After all, they put this here, right? Wrong, again! The recreation center purchased a computer and a system for booking rooms and equipment, but the IT shop made it clear they do not support business applications.

I eventually became a leader in IT, overseeing thousands of applications and a workforce of 5,000 people. At this particular moment in 1998, I had no clue about the inner workings of computers and applications. I didn't grow up using them regularly. If I played a game, it was usually on the family computer. I had just purchased my very own Dell machine (I got to pick the parts) instead of buying a set of encyclopedias, which were about the same price. Based on my training, I knew how to run facilities, manage staff, plan, and direct the work. What I lacked was experience in technology, aside from occasionally fixing the point-of-sale equipment at the dining facilities when it failed. All I knew was this was my new mission.

I needed to determine how this system worked and then figure out how to reserve rooms and equipment, and collect payment. I picked up the phone and redialed the IT department. Yes, even after they told me this wasn't their job. This time, I agreed. In turn, I reiterated to them the recreation center's mission and expressed the frustration we were trying to mitigate. I explained that I now understood the lay of the land and needed their help.

I turned on the computer, opened the application, and found no information related to the recreation center. I needed the IT shop to point me to the information to configure the system.

My story could have ended here. I could have thrown my hands up and said "The team is right, it doesn't work." It was an accurate statement after all and in that particular moment, I didn't know what to do or how to fix it.

But I only like stories that end on a positive note. At this point, I am totally invested in learning why this system doesn't work. It should; it is brand new. It turns on. Why isn't it working?

If you're thinking "just Google it," please understand this wasn't an option in 1998. The computer wasn't even connected to the internet. My work computer was on the base network, but I did not have direct access to the internet. Also, with dial-up connections, everything related to transferring information over the network was painfully slow.

First step, learn about what I am looking at. I am almost desperate to find answers. How does this work? What information does exist? How do the pieces of information relate to one another? If you choose "yes" on this form, what happens three steps later? Without making any changes, learn how rooms are booked and how equipment is rented. How does the application track the collection of money? I had briefly worked as a cashier at a grocery store in high school, and at the start and end of each day, we had to reconcile the cash register drawer. How can I replicate that function within the system?

Second step, try it. Start using the application when a customer requests and books a room. Attempt the same thing in the system; does it work? No, the rooms and pricing need to be configured. Perfect, a clear problem to be solved. Next, I call the IT department, who again reminds me this is not their job, and I agree; I am just asking for information.

Third step, keep trying and calling. I can't tell you how many times I called the IT department, but they eventually put me in touch with the vendor who could answer my specific questions, and collectively we got it up and running. We eliminated the manual process of multiple books and held a little celebration. Mission accomplished. I had no idea this was the beginning of my career in IT.

Unbeknownst to me, the fitness center had the same system, but it was not functioning as the business desired, and errors continued to occur. They also called the IT department for assistance. The IT department had been providing their standard response of that's not our job, except now that they knew I had become a subject matter expert, they began directing the calls to me for assistance. If you'll recall, fixing computers, especially for other facilities, really was not my job. However, the call volume was high enough that, after a while, the IT department made the case to the powers that be that I leave the recreation department and join the IT department. It was a team of three, and I'd be the fourth member, the second person with a military background to join. We worked out of a closet with no windows, filled with servers and network gear, all of which was brand new to me.

I remember the first day I walked into the room. I was entirely out of my element. These people speak in a weird language about system logs, servers, connections, speed, system availability, and access. The equipment itself was intimidating. Basically, I was staring at various black boxes with blinking lights, and the only instructions I received were not to touch them. I was warned of multiple calamities that could occur if any of them went offline, another new term I had to learn. The grumpiest of the guys, but the one who had been most helpful when I was learning the system at the recreation center, barely spoke a word to me other than to give me the various do-nots for working in this tiny space. Do not have open containers of liquid. Do not touch anything besides your keyboard. Do not assume you know; ask questions before you do. He may have even grunted a little before he went back to work.

While he was a bit rough around the edges, I still saw him as someone who had helped me. By this point, I had learned how to work with him. I didn't understand this until much later, but he was responsible for keeping the information flowing for the entire Air Force base via networks and computer systems. It was a significant task, and at that time the role of the technology department was not well understood. When he stopped what he was doing to help train me, it meant there was something else he should be doing. I could understand his reluctance to assist me, but it didn't mean I liked it. However, I became more appreciative of the time he took to share information with me, and I made it a point to show him it was time well spent. If I could take these help desk calls off his plate, he could focus more on what he needed to do. He realized that as well and, more importantly, saw that I applied what I learned each day and I was able to take on more day after day. I didn't go to him with questions unless I had done the work beforehand to learn, and then I only brought him informed questions.

This is another situation where the story could have ended quite differently. I was intimidated by the technology and could have also been frightened away by the gruff team member, but I reminded myself that I had just earned my place on the team. These people, who were reluctant to answer the phone or share information, asked me to join them. They created a role for me, and they advocated to the powers that be that I, a person without a technology background or college degree, should join their team. They believed in me and could see something I didn't, but I saw the door opening, and I walked through it. In a way, this opportunity was a reward for all the hard work I'd put in. I should also mention this did not guarantee a promotion or pay increase. I saw the situation as transactional; I was learning on the job, receiving training that I would have otherwise had to pay for, and I was thankful for the opportunity.

Still, I battled my internal disbelief and constant thoughts that I didn't belong there by reminding myself that I was, in fact, there. I needed to stay focused. This was the first realization that I was becoming more comfortable with not knowing the outcome and trusting my abilities. I could try, fail, and learn. I could rely on my tenacity to keep asking questions, even when everyone was frustrated. I would lean into these skills and continue to fine-tune them. I had been invited to join the team to handle support calls for the system we fixed at the recreation and fitness center. However, I had challenged myself to accomplish more.

Jenn Lorenz

your turn...

Always be learning

Information is literally at our fingertips today. If you want to learn something or acquire a new skill, you absolutely can. In fact there is often too much information; how do you decide what to focus on?

Based on what you want to get done this year, what learning would you focus your time on? What do you hope to gain? How would you apply it to your everyday life or business? Jot down your thoughts on the following pages.

AI Chat Prompt

Consider a scenario where an individual has just joined a project at work that involves a significant technology effort. The individual lacks a technology background. AI can be used to suggest training goals for the year. An AI chat prompt could be this:

An individual without technology experience has just joined a project to implement a new software program for a small business. The job does not require a technology-related background, but the individual wants to know the basics to be able to have more productive meetings and conversations with technical counterparts on the project. Create a weekly schedule that assumes the individual can find up to ten hours a week for training. Note in the schedule how many hours to dedicate to each topic weekly to achieve the training goals. Include motivational quotes to encourage consistency. Include links to suggested training programs and customer review scores.

The AI chat prompt can be adjusted to include specific software or a shorter timeline. Modify it to fit your needs and fact-check the training it suggests. While I have written the prompt to included a customer review score, it is still best to verify directly, especially if you are planning to spend money on the training.

Jenn Lorenz

_____

_____

_____

_____

_____

_____

_____

_____

_____

_____

_____

_____

_____

_____

_____

_____

Jenn Lorenz

Jenn Lorenz

RULE 8
Lead with Respect

"Jenn, I have had it. Sam and Tammy don't know what the *eff* they are talking about. The interconnections between these systems have been built over the course of 40 years. I have been here 30 years and still do not know all of the nuances. To make a change like this, without allowing for proper time to test, is insanity! Also, they are asking *me* to approve and make the change; well, no, I don't approve of it, and the change will not be made. Now they're just wasting my time, asking me to attend meetings to keep rehashing what was already said."

Paul, the system owner, is in my office informing me of the impending doom due to poor planning and decision-making. He continues, "Jenn, I know you're not the project lead, but you know all of these players, and you know where we have to get to. I am on board with the goal to reduce duplicate services, but the approach being jammed down my throat isn't going to work. Plus, my name will be on it as the approver. I simply can't approve of something that I can't explain and that will make things worse. Can you help them understand what is at risk here?"

"Paul, I hear you, I understand your point," I replied. "To move forward, we need all three teams to reach an agreement. I know this is not all on you. Yes, I am aware you are just ensuring that the risks you see are being addressed. I don't think Sam and Tammy are on a mission to waste your time, but let's have this conversation. Your points are valid. Let's see if we can mitigate the risks you are raising."

In this scenario, Paul is the lead of an incredible team that is responsible for keeping the communication between systems operating all day, every day. He has more than 30 years of experience. He is not a fan of changing for the sake of change. He had previously conveyed to me the project is moving fast and there are significant details that are not being accounted for. He has stopped attending the team meetings because he is tired of repeating himself and being pushed to make a change that will cause more harm than good.

The effort has been spinning out of control; no single team has taken charge. Each team is operating in its own lane, focused solely on what it needs to achieve, without much care for the needs of the team that is dependent on them to be successful. Much of what needs to happen is communication-related. I have become the leader of this change effort. I am not the highest-ranking member on the team. As far as seniority, Paul has 25 more years of experience than I do. He is reaching out to me as a cry for help, even though it may sound like a lot of cursing when he vents his frustration.

However, to lead means to go first or show the way. I believe anyone has what it takes to be a leader. Leaders can see where they want to go, and they are ready, willing, and able to create a new path or navigate the one in front of them to get there. I believe showing respect means treating people as you would like to be treated – and it is always my pleasure to be the one who goes first and shows respect to all. Respecting others, honoring your commitments to them, showing them dignity, and listening to their perspective help you inform a positive outcome.

As you know by now, I like to get IT done. Leading with respect is the fast pass there. By acknowledging a person's individual experience and listening to their perspective, you are showing them respect. Incorporating their concerns for all parties involved shows them they are valued and confirms that their time is being well spent. It also gives an outlet to the energy they have, especially in the context of change. If they are dealing with that initial emotional reaction to the change, giving an outlet for their fears to be considered and, more importantly, addressed, they'll get to acceptance more quickly. You will also build trust in the process and deliver a better outcome.

I am a firm believer in supporting the actions that will drive me to the outcome I am trying to achieve. I'm able to put my personal thoughts and opinions to the side. Previously, I described the scenario in Okinawa where the technology lead did not want to give me the time of day. I still called every day. I was respectful each time. Even if the phone call was spent more on him venting about me wasting his time, I didn't give up, and I stayed calm every time we spoke. I found that when I respected his time, understood the nature of the work he was responsible for, and acknowledged it by expressing my appreciation for the time he gave me, I was essentially doing the work to earn his respect. I did the work between our meetings, applied what he had taught me, and made progress.

Over time, he became more agreeable to sharing information, and ultimately, we built a symbiotic relationship. There were tasks that he was good at and tasks that I was good at. He was always going to be a little grumpy and rough around the edges; I was always going to be high energy, filled with hope inside the tiniest room with no windows. Instead of focusing on how different we were or how we didn't understand each other, or how painful it was to work with him every day (I am sure he felt the same about me), we leaned into each other's strengths; after all, the more he trained me, the more interruptions he could ignore. Essentially, both sides got what they wanted; no one person was right or wrong. The measure of progress was simple: the necessary work was getting done in a timely manner. It was a successful partnership, but one couldn't have predicted this in the beginning.

In the beginning, I had every opportunity to argue with him, but where would that have gotten me? He was never going to simply respect me. As far as he was concerned, I was this random person who was making his life difficult. Honestly, he wasn't wrong! I was basically making work for him and hurting his head with all of my questions. I accepted and respected all of it, even though I didn't like it. I didn't like the way he spoke to me. I didn't like how much work I had to do to prepare for a conversation with him. I didn't like biting my tongue and finding a nice way to remind him that there is a better way to talk to people. To be clear, I did use my words to represent how I felt or what I needed to be successful. I just put my energy into respectfully saying these things. This was extremely difficult, and believe me, I was not always the best at it. However, on most occasions when I felt like I wasn't being heard or I wasn't getting the help I thought I needed, I just reminded myself that my opinion didn't matter; what mattered was finding a way to work together and get the job done.

Jenn Lorenz

your turn...

Lead with respect

What are your thoughts about leading with respect?

Can you recall a situation where you felt another person was not showing you respect? Did you respond by showing respect?

If you didn't then, what would you do differently now?

AI Chat Prompt

AI chat is a great assistant in brainstorming ideas. Take the case of Fred, a CEO of a global company, who has learned that a significant project has stalled. The various teams involved will not come to an agreement, many of the individuals state they feel disrespected by their teammates and choose not to deal with each other. The CEO is exasperated and turns to AI chat for ideas to foster respect within the team. An AI chat prompt could be this:

What are some suggestions for leading with respect? What could the first step be to reset the group and operate with respect? What are the potential gains of incorporating respect at this point in time? As the leader, I plan to schedule a reset meeting, create an agenda to facilitate a foundation of respect, and get the work effort back on track.

The results may not fit the nuanced needs of the CEO, but the information can be used as a jumping-off point. The CEO can take the strategies that suit his needs and modify them to include the specificity or timeline he is seeking. The final decision of how to proceed and when will be up to the CEO, not AI chat.

_____

_____

_____

_____

_____

_____

_____

_____

_____

_____

_____

_____

_____

_____

_____

Jenn Lorenz

RULE 9
Go to Grow

What's next, I wondered? I had been in the same position for more than five years. I acquired many new skills, and I was eager to take on additional challenges. I wanted to learn more, do more, and effect more change. I wanted to test the skills I had been practicing with a larger team. I wanted to challenge myself: Could I do a better job of advocating for funding and for an increase in human resources to our upper management? Do I have the ability to make a convincing case and win approval? I didn't know the answers to these questions, but I knew I wanted to try. I wanted to be uncomfortable again and force myself to learn new things. At the same time, I didn't want to leave my team. We had achieved a lot, and we all worked very well together. However, I knew the job wasn't going to change, and the salary was already set, meaning I was not going to get a salary increase if I stayed either.

My only choice was becoming apparent. If I wanted to learn more, do more, and change more, I would have to leave the team that I enjoyed being a part of. It was unfair to expect the business to change the role to fit me. That doesn't make sense from a business perspective. As a business, there is a job to do, and I was hired to do that job. The only change here is me; I wanted to grow.

The old "what are you going to do about it?" record played in my head. Getting it done meant finding a new position. I was intimidated thinking about it. I was searching for a new role that challenged me, that wasn't predicated on everything I had already learned, yet I knew in order to expand my knowledge and capabilities, I *had* to try something new. To encourage myself to take the leap from comfortable to uncomfortable, I reminded myself of my divorce, the first significant change I had to endure early in my life. I reminded myself of all the lessons I learned. I realized I wouldn't have had them if I stayed where I was comfortable. The lightbulb went on; I had to go again. This time, to grow as an individual, and with that, I began to get excited about what could be possible, and I applied for other positions.

The need for this excitement kicked off a pattern for me of intentional professional development. When opportunities or challenges presented themselves, I chose to step up, embrace the change, and challenge myself to learn as much as I could about the role and perform it to the best of my ability. I found that to make room for the new role and responsibilities, I typically had to leave the former behind. To stay when I am not challenged, learning, or driving forward makes me feel like that hamster in the world, running without reason.

My family may tell you that, at this point, I have grown a little too comfortable with the cycle of change, accepting reality as it is, accepting I do not know everything, and being comfortable in knowing I have proven time and time again I will adjust my plan as I learn more. I enjoy the struggles of change now, and learning brings me happiness. Pushing myself has prepared me to take advantage of many opportunities, and my career has flourished as a result.

Jenn Lorenz

your turn...

Go to grow

Consider where you feel stagnant today. Would you like to learn something new? Are you frustrated?

Are you expecting the business to change to meet your needs, or are you willing to seek new opportunities?

Contemplate what those new opportunities could be. Write down the visions as they come into your mind. Do any of them pique your interest? What growth would you experience as a result of going on the path toward one of your visions? Does that excite you?

AI Chat Prompt

A business leader feels their career is not moving in the direction they desire. The leader is comfortable and happy enough showing up to work every day on time and leaving on time. However, they don't feel challenged, and are watching others be promoted around them. A prompt to help the business leader brainstorm ideas might look like this:

Act as a mid-career business leader, not progressing in their career as they had hoped. What questions do people in similar situations have? How does one determine the best path for themselves? What actions could the individual take to change the trajectory of their career? If they had to change jobs to experience this growth, what questions would help them consider the possibilities and risks associated with leaving? List the first three smallest steps for this individual to take in determining their future plans.

Review the results. If you do not find them helpful, modify the AI chat prompt to be more specific to your situation and needs. If the results are close but too generic, use the chat to request more clarification. Remember to verify all information before taking action.

Jenn Lorenz

_____

_____

_____

_____

_____

_____

_____

_____

_____

_____

_____

_____

_____

Jenn Lorenz

RULE 10
Do it Better

"Can you believe it?"

She just made three of our customers so angry that they are calling me, her subordinate, to complain, because I am the only one who knows the nuances of their requests. They also went up their chain because they are unable to perform their daily work. This is a big mistake. She failed to inform them of the upcoming process change and ignored our warnings that this new approach would not be practical for these customers. She was effectively making a decision to lose them as customers, which is well within her rights as the supervisor of the unit. She knows (or should know) what the unit needs to focus on, sets priorities accordingly, and assigns resources. However, in terms of relationships, she could do better. She was new to the unit, having been recently promoted, and was attempting to assert her newfound authority. It's understandable; she wanted something done and dismissed our concerns as complaints from her team. The team warned her multiple times, providing examples and explaining which customers would be upset and why. She chose not to adjust course and refused to change direction in response to the wind.

We were frustrated. We knew we could have avoided this situation entirely. She could have shared her plan with her staff earlier and, where possible, received feedback and adjusted the plan accordingly. She would still be able to accomplish her goals. It just could have been done better. She could have informed these three customers, either in person or by phone call, to gather real-time feedback on what the change would mean for their ability to complete their work. Had she allowed them to do that, we would not be sitting on a call, during the holiday weekend, with our leadership explaining why the change was made and feverishly rolling it back.

After such a failure, she began to micromanage the team. She didn't understand the product the team delivers because she didn't take the time to learn about it. Instead, she focused solely on how our time was spent. When the team was huddled together brainstorming a solution, she couldn't understand why the existing procedures weren't being followed, so she would interrupt the huddle to receive explanations from each member as to why this meet-up was even necessary.

The team was responsible for operations 24/7, 365 days a year; it was always on, not just during the 8 a.m. - 4 p.m. schedule she had earned with her new position. She did not work on call, she did not join calls after hours when something was broken, and she did not provide any expertise to the team. The unit we were in was small, with just eight people. She could have easily taken the time to get to know the team members and their capabilities. She could have used that information about their strengths and weaknesses to inform the decisions she made about work assignments. She didn't even try. The result? Every team member is assigned work as it comes in. True, this is another management style and not necessarily a bad one – but in this case, each person had a uniquely different skill set. Production was set up more like an assembly line, where experts in each aspect of the product simply performed their tasks repeatedly. This new way of being managed created chaos, and the team began to feel increasingly less valuable. Slowly, a silent rebellion began to grow within the team. She didn't notice until it was too late.

She was the newest and highest-ranking member of the unit. I, on the other hand, had been around for a few years, but for all intents and purposes I was the lowest-ranking person on the team. I recalled how I felt when she would admonish the team for the smallest of things, especially during the rollout of significant changes and the ongoing operation of the system. I thought about all the times our concerns were brushed aside; all the work assignments that made no sense, resulting in more work and increased frustration. I watched, cringing, as she was unable to discuss the product we delivered to anyone, not even within her chain of command or to our customers. It was embarrassing to witness. When questioned, her answer was always the same: "I am the manager; I make the decisions." I would think to myself, Why not make informed decisions instead?

I'm not sure why, but the disgruntled workers suddenly stopped doing what she asked of them. They did not say no; they'd agree, but then begin to take a long time to complete tasks (the slow roll I wrote about earlier), if they completed them at all. During this time, I served as the primary point of contact for customers, acting as a negotiator between our manager's directives on how to allocate our time, the staff's current willingness to proceed, and the customer's needs. It is usually easy to work out the details of the task between the staff and the customer, but getting the manager on board was a whole different story.

After a while, she began questioning why the work was no longer coming through her. Why were people listening to me, a lowly employee, and not her? In her mind, the worst part of it was when staff would follow my directions instead of hers. She would constantly complain to our unit head about the perceived insubordination. However, I wasn't being insubordinate; I was informing her and including her in everyone else's disappointment! If she said to stop work, I stopped, but this didn't seem to have any impact. She didn't change her ways, and the team was unforgiving. They shut her out entirely. She ultimately moved on; there was no fanfare the day she left. By the time she had left the team, no one was speaking to her. It was not a good environment to be in, and everyone was glad when it was over – in the end, so much time had been wasted on ego.

I learned two things: First, the people I worked with, both the customer and team, sought successful outcomes. They didn't focus on the amount of time it took to get there. The focus was on providing quality service and quality products. When the team was allowed to deliver, they felt successful; it gave them a sense of purpose, which in turn gave them the energy they needed to keep going. They came to me because I was in the middle and could see all sides and, more importantly, because I listened and would advocate for them with the micromanager, which meant they could spend time doing the work at hand.

The other thing I learned was to stop complaining; it only brought us down more. We would spend too much time dissecting all that was bad, and it would be made worse by our commentary. We were drained by the end of each day. Who wants to work after-hours or put in any extra effort when you feel like this?

From then on, I made the choice to learn from bad managers and people who were disagreeable. I challenged myself to do it better going forward. Whenever I had a supervisor, manager, customer, or worker with habits I didn't agree with, rather than wasting time complaining, I would observe them and pay attention to how they made people feel. I considered whether any of their tactics moved the ball forward or achieved anything. I essentially saw them as lessons of what not to do and challenged myself to do it better. Over the years, I have researched the differences between management and leadership, but I have learned the most through practice.

As I advanced through the ranks, I found ample opportunity to apply these new skills. I listened more, adjusted the plans, and stayed focused on meeting the goal; this provided the team doing the work more freedom on how they delivered the product, and gave them the time and space to brainstorm and solve a problem. Not surprisingly, we ended up with better results and more engaged people. When I was on teams like this, we *felt* like a team. We were in the fight together, doing the work to get the job done.

For this to work, trust is an essential ingredient, and it must be given freely – and taken away when someone breaks the trust by being dishonest or actively working against the team. When trust is present, the synergy is almost magical. The trust is so strong and the members know each other's strengths and weaknesses so well that they automatically compensate for one another in real time. There is no argument about who is doing what. There is only encouragement and support for each member to complete their tasks. Questions are welcome, and cooperation is inherent.

In retrospect, I thank all of the bad managers I have had for so many lessons learned. I was not able to fix their behavior or effectively change the outcomes of their decisions, but I was able to adapt to their style, speak honestly with them and grow from the challenges I felt they created. It is quite possible that all of their decisions are justifiable and accurate. I will never know, but I do know I am better for having had the experiences.

Jenn Lorenz

your turn...

Do it better

I'm sure you've experienced similar scenarios where a person or people have caused frustration and wasted your time. How did you react? Did your reaction help or hinder the team's performance?

Now consider a scenario where you look at them as lessons. Start by writing down what they did that was so frustrating. Now, if you were in their shoes, how would you have handled it differently?

Is this something you can apply to your actions going forward?

AI Chat Prompt

Let's say your supervisor micromanages your time and yet, the team still isn't very productive. Try this AI chat prompt:

Act as an employee who is frustrated by the micromanagement of the team supervisor. Explain why the supervisor may find value in micromanagement. List the pros and cons of micromanagement. Include a list of three leadership books, including customer rating score and link to the description, that inform the frustrated employee how to manage their feelings and provide strategies for navigating the situation in a professional manner.

Review the results, modify the prompt as needed to fit your specific scenario. Adjust the AI chat prompt if further clarification or examples are needed. Did you find some good ideas to use in your own life?

Jenn Lorenz

_____

_____

_____

_____

_____

_____

_____

_____

_____

_____

_____

_____

_____

_____

_____

_____

Jenn Lorenz

Jenn Lorenz

EPILOGUE

Life is hard. Work is work. I have come to expect this will be the case, no matter how prepared I am. A curveball is on its way to my life at some point in the future. The difference now, compared to when I was first setting out on my own, is then I only had enough skills to survive the situation. Today, I thrive. I am confident I will tackle what comes my way. I am comfortable not knowing everything that will happen. I use my fears as fuel to find answers. I choose where I will go, I plan, and most importantly, I "get it done."

In a way, this story ends where it began; new challenges are ahead, and yes, I have some fears. I have embarked on a new journey; after a 20-year career leading technology teams for one of the largest government IT agencies in the country, I have started a consulting business. The pressure is different; my children are grown, and I am only responsible for myself. Regardless, my future self is praying that I make this work! While I planned for as much as I could, there are still many unknowns:, "Will I make a profit?" "How will this new business impact the rest of my life?" "Is this the best way to spend my time?" "How will my work make a difference in other people's lives?"

Only time will tell, but you know what my mom says when I call her with my concerns: "Yeah, so what are you going to do about it?"

I'll leave you with this challenge: the next time you're feeling stuck, overwhelmed, or shocked into a state of despair by unexpected events, give yourself a minute to catch your breath. Then say to yourself, "Yeah, so, what are you going to do about it?"

Snap yourself back to reality by focusing on getting it done, and start with the smallest, least risky of steps. Allow yourself to accept your situation and contemplate the possibilities of different paths you can take. Consider what you truly want or need, and then take that first, least risky step. Use your fears to help you prepare your next steps and mitigate as many risks as possible upfront. Keep going, day after day. Do the work. As unexpected circumstances arise, tackle them with knowledge. Look to what others have done in the past, and how they navigated similar situations. Their lessons may not be an exact fit, but that's OK; you'll adapt the lesson to meet your needs.

When you encounter people who seem to put effort into thwarting your plans, say to yourself, "Yeah, so what are you going to do about it?" You'll continue to get it done by staying the course and not letting negativity drain valuable energy from your resources. Reserve all your energy and time for the thoughts and actions that move you toward your goal.

They say that in life, the only constant is change, and I agree with that. However, the other constant is you. I propose this challenge to you in the hope you will save time and energy, which I consider to be two of your most valuable resources to reach your goals, whether personal or professional. The only person you can control is yourself, and only you can answer, "What are you going to do about it?"

Use the journaling pages that follow to write down your ideas and your plans. What are you going to do about it?

your turn, your rules...

_____

_____

_____

_____

_____

_____

_____

_____

_____

_____

_____

_____

_____

_____

_____

_____

_____

_____

_____

_____

_____

_____

_____

_____

_____

_____

_____

_____

Jenn Lorenz

Jenn Lorenz

About the Author

A lifelong learner, adventurer, and avid problem solver, Jenn Lorenz consistently chooses the road less traveled – embracing the hard lessons and creating great stories for her future self to relive and share. Her latest adventure into entrepreneurship is just beginning, launching Human Insights Consulting Group LLC, a strategic leadership coaching business she is building from the ground up. Learn more at www.insightbyhumans.com.